MATH ON MY PATH

Math in the CITY

Elise Craver

Rourke Educational Media
A Division of Carson Dellosa Education

ROURKE'S **SCHOOL to HOME** CONNECTIONS

BEFORE AND DURING READING ACTIVITIES

Before Reading: *Building Background Knowledge and Vocabulary*

Building background knowledge can help children process new information and build upon what they already know. Before reading a book, it is important to tap into what children already know about the topic. This will help them develop their vocabulary and increase their reading comprehension.

Questions and Activities to Build Background Knowledge:

1. Look at the front cover of the book and read the title. What do you think this book will be about?
2. What do you already know about this topic?
3. Take a book walk and skim the pages. Look at the table of contents, photographs, captions, and bold words. Did these text features give you any information or predictions about what you will read in this book?

Vocabulary: *Vocabulary Is Key to Reading Comprehension*

Use the following directions to prompt a conversation about each word.

- Read the vocabulary words.
- What comes to mind when you see each word?
- What do you think each word means?

Vocabulary Words:

- *addition*
- *analog clock*
- *numbered*
- *rectangles*

During Reading: *Reading for Meaning and Understanding*

To achieve deep comprehension of a book, children are encouraged to use close reading strategies. During reading, it is important to have children stop and make connections. These connections result in deeper analysis and understanding of a book.

Close Reading a Text

During reading, have children stop and talk about the following:

- Any confusing parts
- Any unknown words
- Text to text, text to self, text to world connections
- The main idea in each chapter or heading

Encourage children to use context clues to determine the meaning of any unknown words. These strategies will help children learn to analyze the text more thoroughly as they read.

When you are finished reading this book, turn to the last page for an **After Reading Activity**.

Table of Contents

Math Is All Around

A city is a busy place!

There are people.

There are cars.

There are tall buildings.

If you look closely, you can find math in a city too.

PARK

Numbers in the City

You can find numbers everywhere in the city.

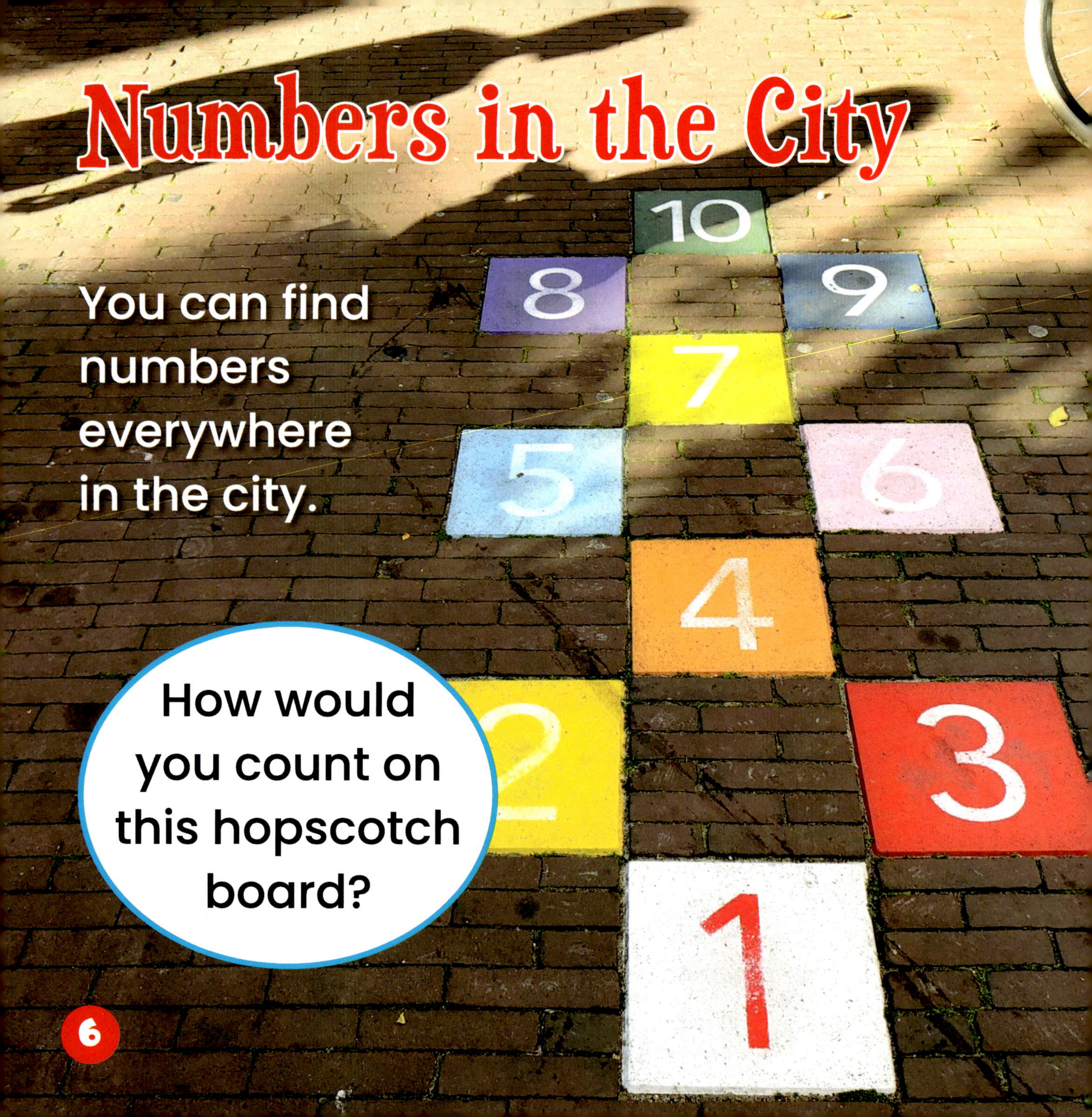

How would you count on this hopscotch board?

Step in an elevator.
Going up!

What can these numbers tell you about this building?

Some kids are playing soccer in the park.

How could you sort them into two groups? Can you make that into an **addition** sentence?

Try it again with these four dogs.

How could you sort and count them in a different way?

Some streets are **numbered.**

What do you notice about these street numbers?

Here is a parking garage.

This sign shows how many cars are parked on each level.

What do you notice about the cars on each level?

Measuring in the City

The subway cars are always running. They have to stay on time. This is an **analog clock**. It uses hands on a clock face.

These times show how long you will have to wait for each train.

Cities have very tall buildings called skyscrapers.

What do you notice about height here?

Shapes in the City

Many people live in the city.

Some people live in houses.

Some people live in apartments.

What shapes do you see in these homes?

There are many **rectangles** and squares in the city. But there are other shapes too!

How many different shapes do you see?

Photo Glossary

addition (uh-DISH-uhn): The adding together of two or more numbers to find how many in all.

analog clock (AN-uh-log klahk): A type of clock with a face and hour and minute hands.

numbered (NUHM-burd): Given a number in order.

rectangles (REC-tang-guhlz): Shapes with four right angles and with equal opposite sides.

Activity: Hidden City Math

Create a city scene using shapes with math surprises hiding underneath!

Supplies

construction paper
scissors
glue
crayons or markers
pencil or pen

Directions

1. Cut shapes, such as rectangles, squares, and circles out of construction paper.
2. Use one piece of paper as the background paper. Place the shapes on the background to create a city scene. Use your imagination! You may create a pond with an oval, a tree with rectangles and circles, or buildings with rectangles, squares, and triangles.
3. Glue only the top of each piece to the background paper to create a flap. For example, add glue only to the top of a skyscraper so it makes a flap that opens from the bottom.
4. Draw on your city with the crayons to create hidden city math! You may choose to draw windows to count on a building, patterns to notice in a sidewalk, or birds to add up in a pond.
5. Under each flap, write the math hidden on that piece of the scene. What math is hiding in your city?

Index

About the Author

Elise Craver is a former teacher who lives in North Carolina. She loves visiting cities, like New York City, San Diego, and Austin. She didn't like math as a kid but loves it now. She and her two kids are always looking for math problems in real life.

After Reading Activity

Have you ever been to a city or seen one on TV? How is the math you may notice in a city the same as inside your home? How is it different?

Library of Congress PCN Data

Math in the City / Elise Craver
(Math on My Path)
ISBN 978-1-73163-840-3 (hard cover)(alk. paper)
ISBN 978-1-73163-917-2 (soft cover)
ISBN 978-1-73163-994-3 (e-Book)
ISBN 978-1-73164-071-0 (ePub)
Library of Congress Control Number: 2020930048

Rourke Educational Media
Printed in the United States of America
05-1252511937

www.rourkeeducationalmedia.com

Edited by: Hailey Scragg
Cover design by: Rhea Magaro-Wallace, Lynne Schwaner
Interior design by: Kathy Walsh, Alison Tracey
Photo Credits: Cover, p 1 ©Arpad Benedek; p 5 ©deberarr; p 6 ©LucyLambriex; p 7 ©Zephr18; p 8, 22 ©JackF; p 9 ©FotografiaBasica; p 10 ©Songquan Deng; p 11, 22 ©Magnez2; p 12 ©Terraxplorer; p 13 ©EXTREME-PHOTOGRAPHER; p 14, 22 ©Xenotar; p 15 ©Devajyoti Chatterjee; p 16, 17 ©gangliulo; p 18, 19 ©Auseklis; p 20, 22 ©alanphillips; p 21 Nikada